My Life Without You

A Mother's Journey Through Grief And Loss

By
Charlene Ross
2022

Copyright © 2021 by Charlene Ross

All rights reserved. This book or any portion thereof may not be reproduced or used in any manner whatsoever without the express written permission of the publisher except for the use of brief quotations in a book review or scholarly journal.

First Printing: 2022

ISBN 978-1-7379629-6-0

Ordering Information:

Special discounts are available on quantity purchases by corporations, associations, educators, and others. For details, contact the publisher at the above-listed address.

U.S. trade bookstores and wholesalers: Please contact info@businessofbooksmastermind.com

DEDICATION

To Symphanie Barrett, Brittany Harris, Khai-Ghiere Harris, Rondell McNair, Ameia McNair, Ethan Drakeford, Storm and Catherine Webb, Detavia Baker, Corey Cotton, Lorenzo "Little Lo" Ross, Jr., Donte Piper, Troy Bailey, and Keith Hagins for their love for Shonquell Barrett.

To Clarence Jackson for being a true friend who came into my life at the right time, believed in me, and pushed me to complete my book.

This book is written is in the memory of Shonquell Barrett and Tahlia Drake.

TABLE OF CONTENTS

DEDICATION iv
PREFACE 6
THE BIRTH OF MY PRIDE AND JOY 12
MY BABY BOY GROWING UP FAST 14
RECALLING AN ACCIDENT 20
DENIAL: REMINISCING ON MEMORIES OF HIM 21
ANGER, BARGAINING, AND DEPRESSION 24
THE FUNERAL 26
STARTING FOR SHONQUELL'S LAW 28
SYMPHANIE'S LIFE WITHOUT YOU 31
PROTESTING FOR SHONQUELL 37
THE FIRST ANNIVERSARY OF HIS DEATH 40
BREAKING 46
COPING IN THE WORST WAYS 50
ANOTHER DIFFICULT CHRISTMAS 62
HAVING A WORD WITH THE GOVERNOR 65
POETRY 66
THE PROCESS OF HEALING 77
REMEMBERING SHONQUELL 81
ABOUT THE AUTHOR 99

PREFACE

In memory of Shonquell (Omelly) Da'Vere Barrett (08/22/95–06/29/18)

My son Shonquell was a very reserved, laid-back guy. Though timid, he always smiled and had a love for all people. He was a big kid at heart whom all the children adored. His memory is a treasure and we loved him beyond any measure. Losing a son is one of the greatest losses in life. It was his end and for me, the beginning to My Life Without You.

On June 29, 2018, the night was warm and still. The sky was one of the most beautiful sunsets I had ever seen. I gazed upon a bright circular opening with soft pink and light blue highlighting the environment around me. Such beauty of the sky that caught my attention.

As I was walking the area taking pictures, I began to have an open conversation with God. I told him that the sky was more beautiful than anything I had ever seen.

"Who are you opening the sky for? Who are you taking tonight?" I asked Him.

Little did I know, two hours later, I would receive a phone call that changed my life forever. It was the call that would begin, My Life Without You.

We often forget certain dates, events, occasions, and many happenings. Then there are dates you will forever remember: the day your son was born and the day he took his last breath.

At 10:03 pm, I answered the phone to a scared, frightened, alarming voice. It was my son, and I could hear how scared and frightened he was.

He kept saying, "Ma, come to me. I'm in a highspeed chase."

I tried to remain calm, but I was breaking inside. The feeling of a mother's intuition hit me in the gut. Then the call dropped. I remained calm and less than five minutes later he called again.

Despite all the noise in the background I could hear him saying, "Ma, just come on, get to me."

The background of the call blared all the more with the whirls of sirens, screaming trouble and danger.

"Son, I am coming," I assured him.

I pleaded to God saying, "Lord, let me get to him."

I instructed Shonquell to go to the corner store and I would meet him there.

"Get to a lighted area. Son, I am coming," I said as the call dropped again.

At 10:13 pm, he called again and repeated, "Ma, please, come on."

"Okay son, I'm almost there. Just pull over," I told him. Believing that he was going to be okay. I sighed with relief.

Detrimental sounds invaded my ear. I was so scared. It seemed like something went terribly wrong. I am talking and talking, and then I scream for my son. It is now 10:20 pm.

"Shonquell, pick up! Answer the damn phone. Please, please answer," I shouted.

I stopped and pulled over, hearing nothing but silence. Realizations bombarded my mind. Occupancy of emptiness, numbness, hurt, and pain have entered with intentions to reside within me.

With my heart racing and mind pondering, I phoned a friend and told him what was going on. He first encouraged me to calm down. I described the details of the horrifying events that led up to the silence of trauma.

"Count to ten," he said. While assuring me. He was giving me hope that everything was going to be okay.

I calmed myself down as much as I could, then went to the hospital where I would meet Shonquell's dad and his sister. Upon entering the emergency room, I asked at the patient check-in desk if my son, Shonquell Barrett, had arrived yet. I explain to her that he was in an accident. She told me that he hadn't arrived, and I started pacing, silently praying, "Lord please let him be okay."

After waiting at the hospital for thirty minutes, Shonquell never came. We started getting phone calls from friends and family. My daughter told me that people were reporting that Shonquell was dead.

My sister called informing me that she and the rest of my family were at the scene along with a representative from a funeral home. She said that I needed to come and identify my son.

I yelled at the top of my lungs, "No! Why is this happening?"

The drive home was the longest four miles of my life. Millions of thoughts were occupying my mind. "Why? Why? Why? This wasn't supposed to happen. He's too young, only twenty-two. I had no last chance to tell him I love him or to say goodbye. Why did my son have to die?" I thought.

I was in total denial, and I didn't know what to do or which way to go. Surrounded by so many people, my body was present, but my mind was miles away. I could hold a conversation, but all I would hear was my son's voice saying, "Ma, just come on," and that loud noise on the last phone call. I couldn't believe that I heard my son's voice for the last time on a phone call.

Now, I must live in remembrance of his smile, his style of dress, his smell. His whole being is now just memories. I knew how to live with him, but he didn't tell me how to live without him. How will I ever learn to do so?

I try to build up an outer appearance of toughness and strength to display. All the while inwardly feeling shattered, broken, beaten, so low that the floor seemed high. This new place of residency for me became dark. There was no light and no shine. I wanted to lay in a fetal position in my bed and not get up for days and days, but I couldn't.

There are too many people who depend on me, especially Shonquell's sister. They were as close as ice and water.

I belted all of my cries and anxieties, being cautious to not unbuckle. I came to the realization that a funeral had to happen. Thank God for both sides of the family because they took care of it for me.

The night before the funeral, I stretched out on my bedroom floor, hopeless, moaning, kicking, screaming, and hitting the floor.

I asked God, "Why did you not give me an opportunity to reach him, to save him as you had always done? What did I do so wrong that you had to take him from me? Oh God, I would have given myself for him."

I had so many dreams for him, so much hope. I can't believe that his dreams were never going to be achieved. My heart shattered from the pain. So many pieces that we can't count or mend, it's unfixable.

I will never have the chance to see him become a husband and a father, to watch him at his sister's wedding. To see his hair turn gray, or to visit his house for Christmas. He would've made the best Christmas dinner because he was a great cook. I always thought I would have more time with him. But that was my plan, not God's plan.

THE BIRTH OF MY PRIDE AND JOY

On August 22, 1995, I gave birth to my first love—my pride and joy. Oh boy, did he come into the world in the most unusual way! At first, the doctor told me that I was having a girl.

Towards the end of my pregnancy, Lord knows, I ate everything! I had the strangest cravings: Cheerios, spinach, and mini-M&M's. And, no, I didn't eat these all at the same time. I know you may be thinking that you're glad of that! Because of my cravings, I gained about eighty pounds.

One month before my due date, my baby still wouldn't turn. This was the hardest part of my pregnancy. The doctor had to mash on my stomach in a circular motion in hopes that it would force the baby into the right position. After an hour of enduring pain, we were getting nowhere. The doctor told me that I would need a C-section because my baby had become breeched. So, we scheduled an appointment for the surgery.

It was August 22, 1995, and I had arrived at the hospital at approximately six o'clock in the morning. Ready to meet my little girl—or so I thought—I was nervous and excited at the same time. The nurses prepped me for surgery and soothed my nerves with calming anesthesia. From the high of the medicine, I was feeling all fuzzy as if I was floating. It seemed like the baby would just slip right out of my stomach!

After they finished prepping me, the nurses said that they would take me to the operating room. As they were pushing me, I started to get a little scared because I had remembered my last pregnancy.

Back then, the baby was stuck in my fallopian tube. I had to have an emergency surgery to remove the baby from the tube, so I lost the baby.

Finally, I had arrived at the operating room.

My eyes were brick-heavy, and I heard the doctor say, "Be very still as we give you an epidural."

I felt some tugging, and the doctor informed me that the baby was still breeched, meaning that it sat in my womb butt first. This breeched position would later explain why they told me that I was having a girl.

At 8:22 a.m., the doctor said, "Ms. Ross, you have a healthy baby boy."

"You told me I would have a girl, but I will love him all the same. Let me see the little bugger that came into the world butt first," I said as I reached out to hold him.

So, I had to come up with a boy's name. At that time, I watched *The Montel Williams Talk Show*, so I went through the alphabet trying to find something that rhymed with Montel. I came up with Shonquell Da'Vere Barrett. He had the finest straight hair and smooth, beautiful skin. He weighed seven pounds and eight ounces and was twenty-two inches long.

Because my son came into the world butt first, we were able to form an immediate bond. He laid on my chest in his snuggled-up position so that it felt like a hug. That closeness between us after his birth brought us together in a special way. When I tell you he was special, I mean it; he was unique all the way around.

MY BABY BOY GROWING UP FAST

Time was flying by, and Shonquell did everything fast. At eight months, he was already walking and dribbling a regular-sized basketball. People watched in amazement as they saw this little boy walking so early. At eleven months, he had an educator's vocabulary.

I recall a conversation that he had with one of my friends in which he gave her some sensible advice. He was watching her as was plugging in a hairdryer.

He told her, "My momma said that you're not supposed to play with sockets, or you might get electrocuted."

She looked at me and asked, "What kind of son do you have? Are you sure that he's only eleven months and not eleven?"

When he was three, one of the mothers from church said something about him that I will never forget. At that time, he was crazy about the not-so-popular Grover from *Sesame Street*. We had a lot of the Grover books, and that woman sat and listened to my son read an entire one by himself.

Afterward, she looked at me and said, "He's been here on earth before, and he will not be here for long."

I could feel myself tightening up, ready to display an enraged madness. What the hell! I was a young mother, and I didn't know how to respond. So, I grabbed my son and proceeded to walk away from her.

At age four, he met someone who would become his whole life and his best friend. I'm talking ice and water kind of closeness. This person was his sister, Symphanie. Since he was an old soul, he immediately became her protector. The first time that he held his sister and introduced himself as her big brother, I knew that he was going to take care of her. The bond that they had developed was inseparable and unbreakable.

By the time he turned the big fabulous five, his intellect was extremely high, and he was reading on a third-grade level. He was incredibly smart, to the point where he would oftentimes take the fun out of things.

One time, he had come home from school all excited, running up to me saying that he had pulled his own tooth at school.

"You should've let me pull it out the special way by tying a string around it, attaching the other end of the string to a doorknob, and slamming the door shut. That way, the tooth fairy would've left you something under your pillow," I told him.

He looked at me with a straight face and said, "No, I think this way was easier."

Sometimes when I picked him up from school, I noticed that he attracted the older kids.

One day when I was getting him, one of the kids said to him, "Alright Quell, I'll see you tomorrow."

When I asked him about it, he told me that it was his friend from second grade. Keep in mind, he was only a kindergartener. At such a young age, he already acted like a grown-up. Here he was, a five-year-old that could iron his clothes. Shonquell was very reserved and laidback for a kid, but he made friends easily. To have known him was to love him. He was so easy to love.

Now he was a slamming seven-year-old with a natural talent and love for basketball. I had envisioned Shonquell playing in the NBA. He had strong arms and impressive skills with both hands. To support his interest in basketball, I became a coach, referee, and sports commentator.

At the end of one exciting game, the coach instructed the team to get the ball into Quell's hands. He came dribbling down the court with fifteen seconds on the clock, needing to make a three-pointer to win the game. Caught up in the excitement, the crowd rose to their feet. As he was coming towards the goal, one of the players fell, laying right in front of Shonquell's path.

His time was running out (fifteen, fourteen, thirteen, twelve), so he jumped over the player on the floor. Then, he got into his three-pointer stance (eight, seven, six, five) and shot the ball. The crowd watched in awe as the ball flew towards the basket and went in just as the buzzer sounded! What a win that was!

Another one of my favorite games was when Shonquell wanted to pass the ball to the whole team so that everyone could make a basket. One of the doctors from a pediatrics clinic had a daughter who played on the team. She was the type of player that dribbled with both hands and threw the ball underhanded to try and get a basket in.

In this particular game, Shonquell kept passing the ball to that little girl, so some of the players were getting mad since she kept missing. So, Shonquell told her that he would block the players for her and then pass the ball. He made a path for her to get a good shot in, passed the ball to her, and, lo and behold, gee-golly, she had made her first basket in the last game of the season.

After the game, the doctor approached Shonquell and thanked him for believing in his daughter. From an early age, my son was the type that believed in giving others a fair chance.

Now he was an excellent eleven; around this time, Symphanie was seven. As he matured, his love for his sister grew alongside his desire to protect her. His love for her was so genuine—the kind of love that others wish they had for their siblings.

When my sister-in-law picked Symphanie up from Boys & Girls Club one day, Shonquell called me at work to verify that it was okay. He wasn't about to let her go anywhere without informing me.

Once again, from an early age, he had always looked out for his sister, family, and friends.

Shonquell was an old soul, and time was flying by. By the time he turned fifteen, he already had the intellectual capabilities of a twenty-five-year-old.

After age thirteen, I rarely saw him open a book. One day, I asked him if his teachers allowed him to bring books home to study.

"Ma, I got this," he told me.

This reassurance was valid. There weren't any teachers calling me about his grades.

When he turned sixteen and was about to start driving, I got a little scared. Oh my, was I an overprotective mom! I wanted to put the squeeze down on him, but I realized that I had to let go just a little bit and accept that was growing up.

My house was where the neighborhood kids hung out, played ball, rode their bikes, and played video games. Shonquell had always made friends easily, so I became the neighborhood mom. Whether it was a birthday or a cookout, the kids came to our house. I cooked for them, but my specialty was always homemade milkshakes.

When Shonquell turned seventeen, he finished school early and planned to go back at a later date to graduate with his class. Out of the twelve years that he was a student, Shonquell had only missed two days of school. He kept good grades and was a member of the National Honor Society, an organization for high school students with a selection based on scholarship, leadership, service, and character. Shonquell met the criteria. Shonquell was also the Boys and Girls Club Youth of The Year and received a scholarship.

When Shonquell's eighteenth birthday rolled around, I couldn't believe how quickly the years passed. He had grown a little mustache and he was a soft-spoken kind of guy, but his voice was getting deep. It was a joy to see him growing up. This would also be the time that God would reveal Shonquell's Law to me.

RECALLING AN ACCIDENT

On a Saturday night in the summer of 2015, there were three young adults in a car--two boys and a girl. The youngest boy was driving the girl was sitting in the passenger seat and the other boy was in the backseat.

As the driver approached a roadblock, he quickly made a U-turn to avoid it. This decision led to a frightening police chase. It would cause the patrolman to perform a PIT (pursuit intervention technique) maneuver. A PIT maneuver is a tactic in which a pursuer forces a fleeing car to quickly turn sideways so that the driver will lose control.

The tactic worked. The driver lost control and crashed into a tree. Out of the three young adults in the car, he was the only survivor. The girl and the older boy, my son Shonquell, died that night.

As I listened to a news report about the chase, I couldn't help but think, "The police should never chase. We need some kind of regulation to implement. Out of the clear blue sky, I spoke of Shonquell's Law, and who knew three years later, I would be fighting to pass a bill, Shonquell's Bill, that would ban chasing and the use of the PIT maneuver in North Carolina.

DENIAL: REMINISCING ON MEMORIES OF HIM

When Shonquell was twenty-one, he was working and saving up to buy his car. At the time, his sister was seventeen, and he drove her everywhere. He even used to sneakily let her drive. This is how they spent quality time together. He spoiled her, taking her out to eat every Friday and doing anything and everything for her.

The two of them had such a special bond. Symphanie was the type of sister that wouldn't eat supper until her brother had gotten home from work. They would always sit at the table and eat together, no matter how late it was. Whether it was nine o'clock or eleven o'clock, she would not eat until her brother was there. The type of love that they had was unbreakable and admired by many.

When Shonquell was thirteen, he always thought he was doing big things. On one Mother's Day, I overheard him waking up his sister so that they could surprise me with a homemade breakfast. He took the lead as the older brother and told her exactly what to do. Oh boy, hearing the excitement in their voices as they whispered about how proud I would be when they surprised me sure did make me feel like a lucky mom.

I laid in bed pretending to be asleep so that I could act as surprised as if Ed McMahon from Publishers Clearing House had just knocked on the door with a big check for me.

That's when I heard Shonquell ask Symphanie, "How long should it stay in the microwave?"

Thinking herself to be as experienced as Rachel Ray, Symphanie said, "Put it in for eight minutes."

I thought maybe they were microwaving something frozen. Then, eight minutes later, I heard what sounded like an explosion. I didn't say anything. Instead, I wondered what condition my microwave must be in and worried about trying to consume and digest my Mother's Day breakfast.

Still pretending to be asleep, I heard their excited little feet approaching my door, giddy and chuckling. When they knocked, I answered with a yawn so that I wouldn't spoil their surprise.

"Come on in!" I said.

"Happy Mother's Day! We have a special breakfast for you!" they said, trying to hold back their giggles.

Symphanie burst out laughing and said, "Shonquell messed up the hotdogs!"

They gave me the tray, and I spotted the source of the explosion; the hotdogs looked scrambled. I had never seen anything like it. Along with the scrambled hotdog, there were eggs, grits, and toast.

Shonquell told me to taste what he made first. Because he had gone through all that trouble, I knew I had to make it seem like it was the best meal I ever had. So, I was chewing and chewing and chewing on the hotdogs. Now, I've never eaten a leather belt before, but I would've bet money that it tastes exactly like that exploded hotdog. Well, it wasn't that bad, and besides, I had a strong stomach.

Shonquell was always loving and had a great sense of humor.

ANGER, BARGAINING, AND DEPRESSION

After the accident, I was overcome with hopelessness. Convinced that I would never recover, I broke down daily. There were times where I would get in my car and drive with no destination. Once, I looked up and realized I had gone all the way to Dillon, South Carolina.

During these drives, I would think, "Why did this happen to me? Why my son? This was too soon. He was only twenty-two. He was so gentle and so kind, with a generous heart that knew how to love. Why did a good person die in such a way? What did I do to deserve losing him?"

I felt as though life had been sucked right out of me. Without him, I was empty and blank. I felt sick to the point that I had to throw up. Something was happening deep inside my stomach, it was moving, turning, and groaning.

The one pain that would disassemble me would be that of his sister. Watching her reaction to the absence of her best friend, watching her understand that he was gone forever—something broke inside of me. Seeing the look of sadness and anger in her eyes, I knew that her pain was deeper than I could have ever imagined.

I asked God, "Why didn't you take me instead?"

I would've traded my life for his without hesitation.

Not knowing what to do or how to feel, I was numb and lost. Sadness filled my eyes. Of the two people that meant the most to me, one was gone and the other was overcome with grief. Though I would have laid down my life for either of them in a heartbeat, I knew there was nothing I could do. There's no use in playing the martyr when the tragedy has already come to fruition.

THE FUNERAL

On the day of his funeral, family and friends gathered in his memory. When I got out of the hearse, the feeling of sickness churned in my stomach as if I was going to vomit. I talked to my best friend, Tracey, who was trying her best to keep me calm. Though I appeared to be listening to her, I was stuck in my head. I thought to myself, "This is so wrong, so backward. I'm not supposed to be burying my son."

Upon entering the building, my water-filled eyes made my vision gloomy and dim. I could feel the heavy grief of his sister, daddy, cousins, grandparents, uncles, aunts, and friends piling up on top of my own. Knowing that I had to be the rock for everyone else, I took a deep breath and held onto my tears.

I had a feeling that, if I broke, everyone else would too. Listening to the stories of my son's family and friends comforted me because I could tell how much he meant to them. Being the proud mom that I am, I wouldn't have expected anything less. Over and over, I listened to testimonies expressing Shonquell's kindness and generosity.

During my final phone call with him, Shonquell told me to tell his sister that he was going to get her phone fixed and that they would get tattoos together. Oh boy, did he love his sister? As I walked hand-in-hand with her, I tried to carry her weight and she tried to carry mine. She gazed at me with vacant, heartbroken eyes. For the entire service, she stayed with me as if we were attached at the hip. I could feel her grief and almost hear her pleas as she wondered why it had to be him.

From the corner of my eye, I could see his grandmother. She was heartbroken, for she knew that she would never again receive a call from him. Even as he got older, they would talk on the phone for hours. His dad let out a cry of devastation, knowing that he would no longer get to hang out with his son.

Then, I had to stand and recount memories of my son to describe the type of person that he was. This day I would never forget. One last look, one final goodbye for now. So many people had come to see him.

It was time to proceed to the cemetery. During the long drive, everyone was in their own thoughts. We rode in silence. Then, we watched the undertakers roll him down to be laid to rest.

I was still in disbelief. I convinced myself that it was all a dream. I wanted someone to tell me that this was all a mistake.

STARTING FOR SHONQUELL'S LAW

The day after Shonquell's accident, news stations from all over were trying to set up an interview with me. Knowing that the news took an interest in the situation aroused my curiosity to the point that I began my own investigation. I researched the PIT maneuver that the police used during the chase. Oh boy, as I was finding out information, I became all the more furious!

Eventually, I found out that there was no probable cause to use the PIT maneuver. The tactic had been carried out unjustly. The police are only meant to use PIT if the fleeing driver is a convicted felon, a committed murderer, or a bank robber. None of these applied to my son.

The policy also stated that the PIT is only justifiable when used in an open field and that it usually calls for deadly force. The chase happened in a residential area and around a lot of trees. Not only did the patrolman that caused Shonquell's accident conduct a PIT in a prohibited location, but he also exceeded the permitted speed limit.

The patrolman chased my son down like an animal and murdered him with the wheels of his car. When performing the maneuver properly, the patrolman should use their car to bump the tail end of the other driver's car, so that it will spin and safely stop.

As my anger and bitterness intensified as I did my research, I immediately turned my hate towards the patrolman that caused the accident.

I wanted to ask him, "Why in the hell did you not call the chase off? Did it make you feel some type of euphoria or power?"

The events that took place that night didn't warrant this type of aggressive deadly force. To me, it was just like shooting a man in the back—cowardly. It was murder by wheels.

Wanting revenge, I dedicated myself to getting justice for my son. I had to find out more about the last moments of his life. I often wonder what he was thinking when it happened, and I feel certain that he wanted me to get to him. He wanted me to save him.

As I learned everything I could about the PIT maneuver, I realized that I must become a strong voice to advocate for my son and others. Along with my family and friends, I quested out to have a protest rally at the DMV (Department of Motor Vehicles), which was the same facility that the State Highway Patrolmen used for their work station.

We walked around the perimeter of the building, chanting, "The PIT maneuver terminates lives! It took Shonquell Barrett's life, and we want justice!"

SYMPHANIE'S LIFE WITHOUT YOU

One month passed, and I was still fuzzy and gloomy, still in disbelief and denial. Logically, I knew that it had happened, but I couldn't help thinking, "This can't be. He was a part of me."

While wrestling with these thoughts in my mind, I was also looking at his sister. I wanted to bear her pain, and I wondered what was going on in her mind. Looking at the brokenness and anger rising in her, so bitter and cold, I knew she must've been in a lot of pain.

She wanted justice for her brother just as much as I did. When I found out about Shonquell's accident, I wished I could've gotten to him and saved him. Here my daughter was, living and breathing in front of me, and I couldn't save her either. I didn't know-how. She was becoming numb and, as I viewed her from a distance, the look of pain that resided in her eyes became something that I would never forget. If her eyes were a book, the title would have been *My Life Without You*. It was causing me to break all over again.

To her, Shonquell was more than just her brother; she also saw him as a dad and as her best friend. She was drowning in sorrow. I prayed to God to allow me to take her pain. Helping her heal was my number one concern.

Remembering Shonquell's Love for Symphanie

The two of them shared a genuine bond of unconditional love. Even when they grew into adults, they were inseparable. The weekend of his death, the two of them had planned on getting their tattoos. Shonquell's would say, "Sister Protector" and Symphanie would say, "My Brother's Keeper."

A memory comes to mind from when Shonquell was seven and Symphanie was four. She was very prissy from an early age, and I often wondered where she got it from (probably from me!). She was also very particular about how she looked.

One day when stopped to get French toast sticks for breakfast, I could hear Symphanie whining to her brother that the syrup was dripping on her clothes. Shonquell took the French toast from her hand and repositioned it so that she could eat without spilling. Looking through the sun visor mirror, I saw and hear her whining again.

This time, the poor child was crying and saying, "It's getting on me brother!"

Back then, she called him "brother" so much that I was starting to wonder if she thought that it was his name.

I kept watching to see what big brother would do in response to all that crying. What happened next melted my heart. He pulled her closer to him, spread a napkin over her lap, and tucked another one into the collar of her shirt. Then, he told her that he would hold the syrup so that she could dip it with his help.

Mind you, she had five more French toast sticks to go, and Symphanie was a slow eater. From then on, I knew that he was always going to look out for his sister.

Another time, when Symphanie was still in a car seat, we were on our way to the park. I always played "Ain't No Mountain High

Enough." I would sing it to them, and we would hold hands and dance. They would get so tickled when I would use my hand as a microphone and go all the way to the floor like James Brown or somebody. That day in the car, when the song went off, it got really quiet.

Shonquell said to me, "Ma, don't be mad or yell or scream, but I think that Symphanie swallowed her ring."

I pulled over to my grandma's house. By the time we got there, Shonquell was crying hysterically saying that he didn't want his sister to die young. I called the ambulance. As the medics were checking her out, Shonquell was asking them if she was going to die.

He was stuttering and crying saying, "S-S-She had it o-o-on the wrong finger."

He felt so guilty as if he had something to do with her swallowing it. The medic was telling him to calm down and reassured him that she was going to be ok. The only thing she has to do was go home and poop it out.

"You are a good brother to have all this concern for your sister. I can see that you really love her," the medic told him.

Then, the medic looked at me and said, "These are some mighty fine children you have."

I had to agree. I gleamed with motherly pride seeing Shonquell's love for his sister. Once again, this situation let me know that he would protect her forever.

There are so many memories that I could share that show their bond, like when Symphanie graduated from high school. Who cried? Her big brother of course. The love that they shared was the kind of love that all people should have in their hearts.

Symphanie's Research Project

Three months went by, and Symphanie had decided to pursue a degree in public speaking at Sandhills Community College. She had to write a research paper and, of course, she decided to write it on the PIT maneuver. Because it was what killed her brother, she dedicated herself to proving that it is a deadly tactic.

When she started her research, she typed her brother's name in the search bar. Lo and behold, his picture popped up and it was a racist site called "Chimpmania." The users on that website are a bunch of racist cowards that hide behind a damn computer to bash black individuals.

They referred to my son as a "coon" and a "disgusting nigger." They said that they hated that the wonderful officer had to come in contact with that "raccoon of a nigger" and that they were so sorry for the tree. But, for them, they said it had ended well because it was one less scumbag off the streets.

Those cowards had gotten pictures from my son's Facebook page and plastered his face all over their site. That was a different level of hurt for me and his sister. Under no circumstance should a site like that exist. I was so glad that my daughter's mind was strong enough to prevent her from committing suicide.

From behind their computers, the cowards did not consider how the horrible things on the website could affect someone else. The things they said were so detrimental that it could cause someone to give up and end their own life. Luckily, my family had always been fighters and overcomers.

Symphanie's Twenty-First Birthday

It was now his sister's twenty-first birthday. I know that Shonquell would have done anything to make it special for her.

As I was walking through the house, I went into Symphanie's bathroom, which is right near her bedroom, and heard her crying. I wanted to help her so badly. She was on the phone, and I heard her say that she was so damn mad that her brother wasn't there.

Ever since we lost him, I had watched her become so bitter, so cold, so angry, and a whole lot of times snappy as hell. I knew that she wasn't resting because I often heard her up late at night. She didn't like being alone, and she lashed out at times.

As I watched her, I could see that she was changing. She used to talk to me about anything, but now she was shutting down and closing me out.

Taking Symphanie to the Doctor's Office

One day I had accompanied her to the doctor's office. This doctor in specific was well aware of the relationship she had with her brother.

When he came in to examine Symphanie, he asked her, "What did your brother mean to you?"

"To me, he was like a daddy, a best friend, and a big brother all in one. I feel like I can't talk to anyone anymore. No one understands how I am inside," she said.

Looking at her outer appearance, she appeared to be so strong. She was just like me, but sometimes I would get angry at her because of the things that I was seeing.

I said to her, "I can't tell you how to grieve or how to cope. What I do know is that your brother wouldn't want you heading down a dark path. It's okay for you to be upset, but he would want you to live and be successful. He's watching you from heaven, so you will see him again someday. Some people are born to live for five years and some are born to live to be a hundred. Unfortunately, your brother was only here for twenty-two years. God kept him here for such a short time because he completed his task on earth. He was born to touch the lives of many. His life wasn't in vain."

"Ma, I'm doing the best I can," she said.

PROTESTING FOR SHONQUELL

Six months after the accident, I still didn't feel like I had achieved justice for his death. All I was thinking was that there must be something that I could do. I decided to have a petition signed at the DMV. I knew I wouldn't feel satisfied until I succeeded.

I called the DMV and told them that I would be facilitating a petition and getting signatures in agreement that the PIT maneuver should be banned in North Carolina. They informed me of the rules for creating a petition.

I gave them an estimate of when I would come to the DMV. I didn't give them a specific date because I wanted the patrolman to see my face, and I was sure that he wouldn't be there if he knew I was coming.

Next, I contacted family and friends, gave them the rundown on what I was doing, and told them what I expected of them. We all arrived at the DMV on a Tuesday morning. On that day, I knew that the patrolmen would be on site.

We set up on a grassy area away from the building, that way we were in compliance with the rules. People were showing up and, as they were signing the petition, a lady approached me and questioned my reason for being there. On the inside, I was ready to bite her head off because I was well aware of my rights. But, I responded to her question in style and with dignity, for I always had great verbal etiquette.

She had what seemed like a hundred questions to ask me. She kept questioning why we were there as if she couldn't see that big picture of my son's car destroyed by the PIT maneuver.

"Listen here. I know my rights, and I'm not on your property. A patrolman murdered my son with the use of his wheels. I am quite sure that you're aware of the incident. I'm here to have people sign a petition," I said to her.

And what did she have to do? Politely turn her ass around and go back into the building. I had four hours to be there and they were going to see my face, my hurt, my pain. They also had to see the face of Shonquell's sister, father, and so many other people who loved him. That look of loss and emptiness became my display when anyone saw me.

The Meeting at the Capital

The time had come to start my quest again, to be heard, to have a voice for my son and others. I called the State Highway Patrol Office and requested a date to rally at the State Capital. My family, friends, and church members got together and carried picket signs at the main building for the patrolmen's office.

After that, I contacted the House of Representatives and requested a meeting with the Task Force, the Department of Public Safety, the senators, and the North Carolina State Highway Patrolmen. My sisters and I looked up statistics and made many phone calls to different cities. We asked if the PIT maneuver was prohibited and how many fatalities had resulted from it.

I was on fire and ready to burn them. I wanted them to feel what I had been feeling and show them how serious I was about my son. I had to break it down to them, so I got prepared. I typed up an agenda and added colored pictures of my son's demolished car from the scene.

When the day arrived, my family and friends accompanied me to Raleigh, NC where I would facilitate a meeting in the conference room. Although I had invited the news station, they weren't allowed in.

It had been 16 months, 487 days, 11,687 hours, and 701,266 minutes without my son. This was my time to talk, and I felt strong and confident in representing Shonquell. It was very quiet, and I had everyone's attention.

I played a clip from the high-speed chase leading up to the PIT. They were listening in awe as they heard the patrolman say that he had to get up to over 55 mph to PIT my son. Mind you, this patrolman was going over 90 mph at impact, and my son was going 55 mph.

THE FIRST ANNIVERSARY OF HIS DEATH

One month before the anniversary of his death, I started to call around to see who had my son's belongings. I also wanted to find out where his car was being kept. After talking to the State Bureau of Investigation and a highway patrolman, I tracked down an officer in Concord. That's where my son's things were. Damn, with these investigation skills, I should have been a lawyer!

I made arrangements to meet at the State Highway Patrolman Office. My daughter and a close friend accompanied me. Although I was driving and talking, at the same time I was wondering what I was about to see. So many thoughts flooded my mind and, upon my arrival, I was starting to feel sick. It was a feeling that you wouldn't know unless you've experienced it yourself. I was also wondering what was going through my daughter's mind as we were about to retrieve the last of his belongings.

We finally arrived and parked. My daughter and I proceeded to get out of the car and enter the building with a feeling of gloom and sadness. I knew that I had to pull it together because I wanted to present myself as a mother of strength and determination who would stand and fight for what she believed in. What I believed in was gaining justice for my son.

My daughter rang the bell and the officer that I spoke with over the phone opened the door. He escorted us down a never-ending hallway. When we got to an office, he asked us to have a seat while he went to get another officer. The wait seemed like forever.

About twenty minutes went by and two patrolmen entered and asked us for identification. Another one came in with a big brown bag that had yellow tape with the words evidence on it. Inside were contents that needed to be verified. The patrolman opened it and started to call out the contents. Everything was in individual bags.

I was listening with a blank stare as he said, "Belt, pair of shorts, wallet, shirt, cash, earring, three dimes, and two pennies."

Looking through blurry, tear-filled eyes, I saw dry blood on his shorts. I immediately turned my head as the patrolman put the items back in the bag. This was something that I wanted to do in private.

I looked at my daughter as she was watching the patrolman. Both of us were thinking the same thing. I got the bag and, when we returned home, I put it in my son's closet until I was ready to look at it again.

One week had gone by, and I decided that it was time. I opened the bag and pulled out the contents: a blood-stained t-shirt that was ripped off of his body, shorts that were cut off of him, and his belt that was torn in half. I was mad and hurt, and I felt myself getting sick. I put everything back until a later time.

Two weeks before the anniversary of his death, I called the patrolman to see if I could get access to see my son's car. This would be the first time that I would get to see it since that night that he left the house. My daughter and I arrived at a towing place, and I located his car.

I was in disbelief to see the condition that it was in. I was looking to see if there was anything that I could get to salvage. I had no words as hurt covered my eyes. I wanted to fall on my knees and just scream my ass off.

June 29, 2019, was the first anniversary of his death. I had a balloon release with family and friends. I was still feeling like the accident had just happened. Many of his family and friends came to honor Shonquell. Hearing all the different stories from his classmates and closest friends was a refreshment to my soul.

One of his friends had shared a story with me. He said that he had called Shonquell and asked him for five or ten dollars for gas to get to work. Thirty minutes later, Shonquell pulled up and gave him twenty-five dollars and told him that five or ten wouldn't get him far, but twenty-five would get him through the week. He had a generous heart that was so similar to mine.

Another one of his friends shared a story with me. This boy had been living from pillar to post, so he didn't have much. He had been wearing some old beat-up sneakers for a long time and told Shonquell how bad his feet were hurting. My son asked him what size shoe he wore and two hours later, Omelly (a nickname for Shonquell) came back with a pair of Jordans. The young man was teary-eyed as he shared his story with me. He said that nobody had ever done anything like that for him before and that he appreciated their friendship. Anytime someone approached Shonquell with a problem, he wasn't the type that would tell you no, but rather, he would find a way to help.

My favorite story was from one of my son's classmates who approached me with a hug and held on to me for a little bit. He told me that, after losing Omelly, he changed his life around. He went back to school and bettered himself to show his younger siblings that he could do it. If you ever came across my son and talked to him, you definitely would like him right away. He had that type of good vibe and was a true friend for life.

Once the anniversary passed, I went back to feeling sad, depressed, and lifeless. In a very dark place, I was giving up and saw a point of no return. I was drowning in grief, and I had to muster up strength just to take a shower, only to lay back down in a bed full of sorrows.

Moaning and groaning in agony, I started kicking my legs and having an argument with God, "Why? Why? Why? Why? Why did you take my son from me? I would have sacrificed myself for him in an instant. What did I do to deserve this? God, why didn't you understand how much I loved my son?"

Four days passed and I hadn't eaten at all, so I decided to phone my sisters. But, what could they say to me that would even matter at this point? They were trying their best to find the right words and scriptures.

Both of them went into prayer mode to the tenth power and, out of nowhere, a huge fly mysteriously appeared as if from another planet. When it started buzzing in my ear, the sun made its bright entrance. I looked like Bill Bixby turning into the hulk when the brightness shined in my eyes. The fly just kept on buzzing and buzzing. It was so annoying that I had no other choice but to get up.

I was so thankful for my family. It was like my world had stopped all around me but life kept going. Days kept coming and passing by. A person can't understand this hurt until they've felt it themselves. Living after a tragedy of this degree requires constant coping. The one thing a person should never do is judge someone else's pain.

Knowing that I had to pull myself together, I showered, got dressed, and decided to go for a little ride. When I stopped for gas, I saw a little girl who was about seven years old. I recognized her from Shonquell's funeral.

She approached me, poked me a few times with her little finger, and gave me a hug. Wouldn't you know, God was still working behind the scenes! She looked at me with her bright eyes and told me that my son Omelly was her best friend. I told her that he had a lot of little friends her age, for he had a special gift with kids. He was so loving and would've been a great father.

BREAKING

I was feeling like I hadn't accomplished anything to gain justice for my son. Eighteen months flew by so fast. I felt like a failure—frustrated, hurt, despaired, weary, useless, helpless.

I watched my family members and some of my son's friends struggle to cope with his untimely death. The different levels of pain that I saw were deep and unimaginable, but I felt that my grief was magnified a hundred times over.

I had nothing more to give. Even though I had family and friends that had lost a child, I felt like I couldn't relate to anyone. My pain was different. It was like I was the only one that had experienced this type of hurt. You couldn't understand this kind of brokenness until you've experienced it. It's like you have to give "break" its own identity.

Receiving Hate at the Scene of the Crime

I came across some of the rudest people I had ever met in my life, and I was seeing it up close and personal. There was no compassion or love when all that should've mattered was that a mother was without her son and a young man was gone from his family forever.

In the aftermath of the accident, my dad accompanied a news team to the site where it had happened. The tree that my son crashed into was in front of a lady's house.

This woman came running out of her house screaming, "Get the fuck out my yard! Your son is dead, and there's nothing that you can do about it."

I was furious. So many people had left teddy bears and balloons at the site, but this mean woman didn't give me anything. This was a big hurt for me. I wondered, "What if the shoe was on the other foot?"

I knew that not once did her pea brain think of such things. She wouldn't understand how kind gestures would help us cope, but she was a mother just like I was.

My humble sister said to the woman, "Ma'am, have a nice night. I hope you sleep well."

The next day, the woman put up a "No Trespassing" sign in her yard. Family and friends were calling to tell me how she ran them off her property. One thing for sure is that, when people show you who they are, you should believe them.

Hearing a Sweet Story from Shonquell's Co-worker

On a warm Monday afternoon, I got home and checked the mail to find a letter addressed to Symphanie from her brother's employer. Apparently, he had a savings account set up while he worked there which had his sister as the beneficiary. I told Symphanie that her brother was still looking out for her. Even after his death, he made sure that she was taken care of. Once again, Shonquell expressed the love that he had for his family and friends.

A man that worked with Shonquell shared a memory with me. He said that he and my son would often talk about life. One time he told Shonquell that he felt like giving up because life sometimes seemed so unbearable. The man told my son that he wanted to drink away his troubles.

Shonquell said, "Where on earth do you think your troubles will go once you drink them away? If you think like that, at the end of the night, the only thing you will accomplish is alcohol consumption, a hangover, and a headache. By the morning, your troubles will still be there. You need to face your problems one at a time. Day by day, you'll be one step closer to creating the life you want."

Here in front of me stood a forty-four-year-old man.

He said to me, "I had no idea until Shonquell's death that he was only twenty-two because he was so full of knowledge and wisdom. It was as if he had been on earth for a long time. I could always talk to him, and he would help me see things differently."

Running into Shonquell's Elementary School Teacher

One day, I was sitting in my car and leaning my head back with closed, teary eyes. I heard a little tap on the window and, when I looked up, I saw my son's teacher from the elementary school. She told me that she had been trying to contact me to extend her condolences. She thanked me for raising such a well-mannered and respectful son and told me that his smile had oftentimes made her day.

Then, she recalled how he would hold the door open for her. When she was coming from far away, she would see Shonquell holding it open and think that there's no way he would wait so long for her. But, of course, sweet Shonquell waited until she walked through the door. She thought that the only explanation for his kindness must be the way he was raised.

I thanked her for sharing that story. It reminded me once again of how special he was and how he not only improved the lives of others, but he touched their hearts too.

COPING IN THE WORST WAYS

I was living in a dark place. I struggled to sleep and, before I knew it, a whole week had passed with me only getting a few hours of shut-eye. On top of all those, my body started going through menopause.

Nobody knew that three years before losing my son, I was three days from turning fifty. Around that time, the state came in and shut my job down. That same night, my car was repossessed. My son's accident happened two months later.

I began questioning God, "What are you doing? This was no way to be turning fifty. Why am I going through so much? I'm a good person. God, I know that you can see that. Why would you take my son? He mattered so much to me. He was my first love, my firstborn."

At that point, my son's voice echoed in my ear saying, "Ma, just come on and get to me."

That's what my son kept saying on the phone that night. It echoed so much in my ear, in my thoughts, and in my head.

The journey that I would have to walk through would cause me to see myself as ugly and worthless. I was becoming someone that I no longer recognized. I was seeing myself at my worst.

I had so many emotions that would introduce—or shall I say re-introduce—some things that I engaged myself in back in my past. Because I was having a hard time sleeping, I first introduced myself to Tito's Vodka.

Before, I was never one to drink alcohol because I didn't like the taste. If I did drink, it had to be fruity or just some simple wine. One day, I stopped by the liquor store and got four of the individual bottles of Tito's. I tried it with Sprite, but that wasn't it for me, so I poured it out. The next bottle I tried with orange juice, and that wasn't it either. Now, this wasn't any cheap liquor for me to keep pouring out.

Then, I decided to try it with fruit juice. Hot damn! B-I-N-G-O! This was the drink for me! It had a great taste, so I learned how to mix it and make it taste like Kool-Aid. I would have four or five drinks a day and, for the first time in a long time, I slept for four hours straight. Most of the time, I was only getting four hours of sleep for the entire week.

This would go on for about four months. At first, it was only once a week, but then I started doing it twice a week, and then damn near every day. The bottles had started accumulating, so I hid them in the cabinets because I didn't want my daughter to see them. She never saw me bring alcohol into the house; it was something that I just didn't do.

I started buying the giant bottles to save money, and they would last longer. It seemed like the more I bought, the more I drank.

Trying to Survive Christmas

Christmas was coming up. The first Christmas was the hardest, but none of the holidays were easy. On top of all that grief, I was lonely and had bad mood swings due to menopause. There were times that I felt like I was bi-polar; I was up, down, up again, down again.

At times I was wondering, "What gave me the right to smile, have fun, enjoy myself, or continue living without my son?"

Trying to be happy without my son didn't feel right, and I don't know how to live without him. My life stopped after he died, and there were no more fun days. I felt myself drifting down and spiraling into the unknown. It was a place that was dark and gloomy—a place that had no life, no sunshine, only blackness. I was starting to wrestle with the thoughts in my mind, and I would come out the loser every time. My bizarre behavior would last for another six months.

On Christmas, I woke up empty with a heaviness of gloom settling in my eyes. Sometimes, my mind would become quite fuzzy as I tried to wrestle with all my emotions.

My daughter had gotten up, and I heard her coming. I knew that I had to straighten up, so I proceeded to get up and fix breakfast. With the way I was feeling, I knew that any type of negativity would set me off.

My daughter and I planned to have Christmas breakfast at my cousin's house. Upon my arrival, I saw a lot of my family was there. I went inside and was greeted at the door by my daughter. We planned to exchange gifts there as well.

As my daughter and I exchanged gifts, all I could hear was my sister saying, "You have a daughter left, and she needs her mother."

My eyes filled with tears, and I couldn't speak. I had no words, absolutely nothing. I did my best to muster a broken-sounding "Merry Christmas." After I gave my parents their gifts, I could no longer remain in that environment with everyone. I immediately left because I could no longer hold back my tears.

All alone, I returned home and watched videos of my son. I sobbed and shouted at God with anger. I started to drink and drink and drink and drink. This time, I had overdone it. As I became drunk, I was throwing up and my head was spinning like a merry-go-round.

I tried moving my head from side to side and holding my head still, but nothing worked.

I started praying and pleading to the same God that I had previously had a shouting match with. I begged Him to make it all go away and was wondering how other people could like this sick, woozy feeling.

The alcohol was nothing but a downer for me. I finally drifted off to sleep. The next day, the only thing that I had accomplished was a bad headache. This is when I realized that drinking wasn't getting me anywhere and that the devil was trying to get me to think that I needed alcohol to go to sleep.

I was going through my laundry to sort my clothes. As I got towards the bottom, lo and behold, I had bottles tucked away in the basket. There were twenty-three empty individual drink bottles of Tito's.

Then, I walked into my kitchen to get some pears from the cabinet. There it was again: another scene. If it was in a movie, the title would be "The Liquor Cabinet." This drinking habit was looking very ugly. Who was this stranger that I was becoming?

Questioning Myself and My Drinking

One night, I went to a party where I knew some of the people. Because it was a party, I decided to take a drink. I had an audience at my throat.

One of the ladies said to me, "Hi Char. I didn't know you drink. I thought that you were a Christian."

In my mind, I was thinking, "Who in the hell made a law that you can't be a Christian because you have a drink?"

This lady went on to tell me how she remembered me from school. She said that, back then, I seemed quiet, sweet, and innocent—the kind of girl that never got in trouble.

I was sitting there wishing she would just be quiet. She didn't know the thoughts that were running through my head.

"I'm still sweet. The alcohol doesn't affect who I am," I told her.

Hell, I was only having one drink!

"I appreciate your concern, but I am just fine," I said to her, hoping that she would get off my back about it.

This experience taught me that there are people watchers who observe you and expect to see perfection. Then, when you slip up, they call you out on it. The way this lady talked to me let me know that her expectations of me were high and that my behavior wasn't matching up. This is the kind of person that I usually like to avoid.

I could still feel her eyes on me as she was watching to see if I'd have another drink. I was holding my tongue and hoping that she would just sit herself down and stop staring at me, I rolled my eyes at her. Even though I knew that she would be thinking that I'm an alcoholic, I spared myself from worrying about her opinion of me.

This lady's concerns about me weren't worth my time, but the interaction did make me wonder what other people were thinking. I started to question if I had let the important people in my life down.

"What if I'm failing my daughter's expectations?" I thought to myself.

Wrestling over this question hurt because if there was anybody who believed in me, it was my daughter.

I always wanted to present myself as a strong person so that I could be someone that inspired others. One thing is for sure; a person can never say what they would do in a situation like mine until they've experienced the brokenness themselves. I used to always hear people say what they would do if they were in another person's shoes. For example, someone might say, "Oh girl, that couldn't have been me. I would've left him!" or, "Look! Now she is in that bottle."

People say these things with no understanding of the true extent of the brokenness, pain, deceit, and betrayal. No one's pain is the same and no one handles it in the same way.

The pain behind the addiction couldn't possibly be understood by this lady who was judging me. I got a mouthful of this kind of experience at the party. The little comments that she made to me that night really caught my attention.

Finding Symphanie's Hidden Pain

One day, on the way home from work I stopped to get groceries and a pint of Tito's. When I got home, I started carrying the bags from my car into the house. My hands were so full that I could barely unlock the front door. Once I finally got it open, some force led my feet straight to my daughter's room with all the bags still in my hands. What I saw when I opened her door would be another break to my heart. I saw several empty bottles of alcohol. It caused me to fall to my knees. I saw just how bad my daughter was hurting. The things that I was hiding from her, she was also hiding from me.

These were the empty bottles I found in my daughter's room

I was so worried about Symphanie, so I started to pray, begging God to spare her life, watch over her, and keep her safe. The pain exhausted me. I didn't know what else to do except pray. I started to pace the floor from one end of the house to the other.

I talked to God and said, "My son is already gone. Please, don't take my daughter too. Don't let anything happen to her."

Then, I called my sister in Georgia and shared my feelings with her. We talked for a short time because she didn't have much to say. A few minutes later she sent me a song to listen to called "Something Has to Break".

It got dark, and I prayed like never before. I felt like, if I got on my knees, God would know that I meant business. Over the next four weeks, I read my Bible more and prayed throughout the day.

It was a Thursday night, and I was stretched out on the floor in a fetal position as I rocked back and forth.

I asked God, "Why am I going through all this hurt and pain? What am I supposed to be doing?"

On that night I would get a divine visitation from Jesus. In my dream, I was standing outside taking pictures of the moon. The moon was so big and bright. It was amazing, and I was in awe. As the moon moved through the clouds, a man with a guitar came down from the sky along with another man on a horse.

Floating towards me was the most beautiful white cross outlined with ridges. It was pure and wholesome. When the cross was coming closer and closer, shining exactly where I stood, I could say that Jesus was on it. He floated straight to me and extended his hand out. I gave him my hand but snatched it back quickly.

Jesus extended his hand again, and this time I gave him mine without pulling away. The touch was so real, soft, gentle, and smooth. Jesus floated around me and told me to write this book. He said to start with Genesis, which would be Shonquell's birth.

Jesus looked at the man on the ground and said to him, "Read the book because it's going to be good."

Then, they floated back up to the sky.

I woke up rubbing and feeling my fingers. It was the most wonderful feeling in the world. I began to meditate on my dream. One week before, my best friend Tracy had called me and said, "Char it's time for you to write your book. You should start from the beginning when Shonquell was born."

"I don't know how to write a book. I only know how to write plays," I said.

"God will give you everything you need as soon as you start writing," she told me.

My encounter with Jesus and my best friend's support confirmed that I should start writing about my experience. It doesn't get any clearer than that. I started with Genesis, the birth of my son, just like they told me. Eventually, I got distracted and deceived in the worst way, which set me back as I procrastinated.

ANOTHER DIFFICULT CHRISTMAS

When Christmas rolled around again, I knew that I didn't want to feel the way that I did on Thanksgiving. I was still not in a good place, and I didn't want to be alone for the holidays.

A few days before Christmas, I decided to go to a party. I'll be damned, there was a blunt getting passed around! The alcohol that I had consumed got into my head and told me to take a few puffs from the blunt to see what my daughter felt like when she smoked it.

It was being passed my way, and they skipped over me because they knew that I didn't smoke.

"Let me try it," I said.

I took three tokes and went to sit down. For about fifteen minutes, I sat there thinking, "What in the hell is going on?"

My legs wanted to move on their own without me controlling them. I felt myself getting sick, and I immediately went outside. I didn't want to lose my dignity.

My friend called and asked me where I had gone. I was sitting in my car and I told her that I felt funny. I couldn't describe the feeling, but it wasn't good. When she asked me what happened, I told her that I took a few puffs off the blunt.

In a firm voice, she asked me why I did that because she knew that I didn't smoke. She told me that it was some kind of weed called "loud."

"Whew! Well, I just didn't want to feel like I did on Thanksgiving," I told her. That's all I could say to try and explain myself.

This was the very first time that I wasn't able to drive my car. I would have to go home, and my daughter would see me in the ugliest way. I knew that I was going to have to tell her what I had done, and I felt like the scum of the earth.

I arrived home, and my stairs looked like mountains. On top of that, I didn't have any rails to hold on to. I made it straight to my bathroom and threw my guts up. Standing right there was Symphanie. I started to tell her what had happened. What she said to me would cause me to look like a fool.

My daughter was looking at me as if to say, "What in the hell is wrong with you? You're supposed to be my momma, and you're out here behaving like this?"

As I braced myself for her judgment, it shocked me to hear what she actually said. She promised that no one would ever find out and that it would be our secret. Then, she ordered me some food and helped me get in bed.

"It was just an experience that I went through. I'm going to be open and honest about my journey through grief. Still, you shouldn't smoke that garbage," I told her.

Before she left me alone, she made sure that I was okay. I reassured her that I was going to be fine and that all I needed to do was throw up a few more times.

When she finally left for her friend's house, she called to check on me every thirty minutes. I finally had to tell her that I could go to sleep if she stopped calling so much. Before I hung up, I thanked her for her help and told her how much I love her. I felt so bad for making her worry. After that, I knew that I had to pull myself together. I could no longer let my daughter down.

HAVING A WORD WITH THE GOVERNOR

I had one more meeting with the Governor and his staff, and it would have to be done virtually. They informed me that I would get twenty minutes to make my case, and I prepared very well for it. The facilitator called my name, summoning me to the meeting.

All of a sudden, they told me that I had two minutes, so I didn't have time to blink on them. Pushing the time limit, I said everything I wanted to say. When they told me that my time was up, I was able to squeeze in one last thing.

"The two minutes that you gave me to speak was the same two minutes that the patrolman could have used to save my son's life," I said.

This is the line that they would remember me by.

From A Mother's Broken Heart

Emotions and tears that I've kept tucked away and bottled inside,
It's been 10 months since you left me.
I still ponder what could I have done differently for you to still be here.
One of those days so much unsaid so much unspoken,
Sometimes torn, sometimes broken.
The silent prayers that I prayed for you,
Still, God took you.
I've mastered the look of strength and I wear it well,
If this picture could tell a story of hurt and pain.
Although I lost you,
You had everything to gain,
A perfect place of peace, a new home in the heavenly sky
For silent tears, I still cry.

Love, Mom

My Brother

My brother and my best friend, unknowingly that
June 29th would be the end.
I will miss your laugh and your big smile,
It's unreal that you couldn't stay awhile.
Without you, I feel lost and all alone,
God picked you and took you to his heavenly home.
Lost to the quickness of time, I'm mad and angry
Wishing I could push rewind.
You always asked what we would do without you?
Now our hearts are broken into two.
Cold, cold world dark and blue,
Our hearts weren't ready but God chose you.
My heart, my world, my partner
My real "right man" I'm going to miss you!
Your Best Friend,
Symphanie Barrett
Sister

From My Heart

Shonquell, my firstborn, my first
Welcome to heaven above.
Who knew this day would be that you would leave me?
That beautiful smile that I will forever still see.
The pain inside, Oh I'm feeling so empty.
You went too fast, you went too soon,
Now we're planning your funeral this Sunday afternoon.
You were kind and gentle with a big loving heart.
Not fair that you had to depart.
My heart is hurting because I loved you so much.
No feeling, just numb to the touch.
As my throat lumps and my eyes fill with tears,
I only got to keep you for twenty-two years,
My soul cries out "Shonquell" with a shout,
Mama loves and will miss you no doubt.
My firstborn, my first love,
Now enter into Heaven above.
Love, Mom

My Son

Last night I entered your room,
Overcome with gloom
Searching for answers to questions
Thinking it should have been me
As I sat on your bed and begin to look around
So quiet without sound.
Remembering the music, you use to play that I didn't care for,
Now I would love to hear just once more.
As I pulled back the curtain to look out the window
Seeing a vision of your face and I'm watching you drive away for the very last time, Not knowing your home would be a new place.
Going through your clothes, recalling your style of dress and that beautiful bright smile.
That stayed on your face. Only if I had stayed home longer at least for a little while.
Could it have been different would you still be here?
My heart shattered as though I'd been hit with a sphere
I will never know or understand
Only God knew the plan.
Love, Mom

The Final Call

I loved you the best I could beyond measures
Your life was more valuable than any treasure.
It was June 29th, you were driving your white Honda,
You decided to make one more call to your Momma.
What was going through your mind?
What was pondering inside your head?
You did not know that you'll end up dead.
The plan was to meet you at the store,
Thinking that I'll see you and it would be forevermore,
Thinking that I'll get another chance to love you a little harder,
I could hear the siren as they got louder.
I could tell they were getting closer to you,
My mind and heart were racing and I didn't know what to do.
I had to phone a friend cause I felt like it was the end.
He told me to take deep breaths, to pull over, and calm down.
He said that he would pray.
As it would be I wouldn't get to see you the next day.
I received a text that said Moore County Man Dead after chase
I miss seeing your smile and your loving face.
Missing you son
Love, Mom

Son

What is this that weighs on me, this heaviness that's causing me not to rise?
A force that's holding me back
Can't move stuck and glued to the bed.
Oh, the thoughts inside my head
Emotions of hurt and pain that's causing me to sob and weep.
What is this that has me bound and weak?
What is this? A mother's cry who didn't grieve
When she had to say goodbye.
What is this? it has a name
It's called depression and it's rebuked in Jesus' name
Love, Mom

Unsaid

Still, there was so much that I wanted you to know,
Still pains me that you had to go.
Still so much that I wanted to show and tell you,
Only with God is how I'm getting through.
Assuming that you would always be there,
Still seems too much to bear.
Never did I think or have a clue,
That I would have to live my life without you.
For days and days, the sun doesn't shine,
No brightness, sometimes dark clouds or morning dew.
Each tick-tock turns into time without you,
Traveling through grief wasn't the ride I had in mind,
God made you special, one of a kind.
If I were a bell, I'd ring all the way to heaven,
I'll tell you that you were my everything, my all and all
My life without you will never be the same, God made the Final call.
Missing you son, until we meet again.
Love, Mom

Sleepless Night

Restlessness, awakened by deep pain and hurt in my heart.
When my thoughts are too heavy,
My feelings too numb, when my heart is unsteady and the tears start to come, Thoughts of swirling anxieties pressing heavy.
Peace seems so far away, so unreachable.
I long to fall asleep,
Missing you son, I loved you then,
I love you still
I'll see you again, I know it's God-willing…
Love, Mom

A Shattered Heart

A place that reaches the unknown
A shattered heart, a loved one gone.
Grief changes everything, your entire life.
No more normalcy, how do we live?
How do we go on?
Each awakening day still comes with the memory that you're forever gone.
No end to a loss
Still, those days come and I don't want to get out of bed.
This is no nightmare or some bad dream, although it seems.

No chance to ask God to switch places The hurt of pain shows on faces.

In quietness I wept, I would have laid down my life so you could've been kept.

In agony I moaned, my son is forever gone

I've had some highs, I've had some lows.

I picked up some habits and you are very missed

only if I could've given you one last kiss.

I've had some dreary days and I've experienced some deep dark places.

A shattered heart, broken into pieces.

Love, Mom

Secretly Within

I never knew how broken, how hurt,
People say she is so strong,
blind to her pain that lies within.
Always loving, always kind through her madness of pain,
Untimely emotions, her restless nights,
Sometimes sad, sometimes depressed,
Her daily struggles to get up and go,
Hiding it well, and if she tells, is the only way that you will know.
I've seen her grow; I've seen her fall.
Mind reflecting on that night when she got that final call,
She's secretly within, how do I know? Because she is me.
Having God-given power to say that this is not how my story will end.
The Master created me not only to fight but win
Missing you son
    Love, Mom

THE PROCESS OF HEALING

Give yourself time to process your grief. Never let someone tell you to get over it and move on. It's never okay to tell someone that. One thing about grief is that it doesn't have a time limit or an expiration date.

At one point, I avoided my grief. I did everything I could to not cry at the funeral. By doing this, I let myself become angry and bitter. I didn't give myself time to process it.

All I knew was that I got very busy trying to find ways to honor my son. The only thing I wanted to do was to prevent his life from ending in vain.

I once had a conversation with another mother who had lost her son. We shared some memories and cried together, not knowing that we had an ear hustler that was listening to our conversation.

Out of the blue, the voice of a jack in the box mouth echoed the statement, "Why are y'all crying over your sons?"

Jeanne went on to say that she stopped crying over her son. She believed that God had only loaned her son to her and took him back so that she could have her pleasure. What she said went over my head, and I walked away.

However, the idea kept bothering me so bad that I had to say something. I approached her and asked if I could speak with her briefly.

"One, you don't ever tell someone that they can't cry over their child," I told Ashley.

What she said next would almost cost her a beat down. She told me that I was weak. It took everything for me to keep it together. I wanted to slap dust from her face.

"God has got me so strong right now because he's allowing you to keep your damn teeth. But since you are trying to take me there, we can definitely go there," I said to her.

This caused her to get out of my face. I told her that I was done with her and demanded that she stop talking.

I went home and prayed. There was no way that this woman knew what she was talking about. After I prayed, I realized that this woman was hurting so bad and didn't even know it. I felt as though God sent me to her to help her heal.

Taking time to cry and let everything out, I started journaling about anything I thought of. I wrote down my feelings, some good and some not so good. After all that writing, I began to release a lot of things that were bottled up. I also got angry at my son for leaving us.

A lot of nights, I had loud conversations with my photos of him. I let him know that I was angry, but I also blamed myself for not being able to get to him, to save him like I always had done. To sum it all up, I also became angry with God, and he was expecting me to be angry with him.

God said, "In all ways, acknowledge Me."

This let me know that it was okay to ask God why He took my son and to wonder how I was supposed to live without him.

I felt like I didn't deserve to smile or be happy ever again. How could I? My son was gone.

God reminded me that many wouldn't know how I felt or would even begin to understand. God let me know that He knew my hurt and pain because He lost His son too.

It's also okay to get involved in a support group. I thought that I was the only one that had this kind of pain and that nobody could identify with what I was feeling, but I was wrong. There are people going through the same thing that you're going through. It's someone else out there that needs to hear your story.

There were times that I had to find a different outlet, so I started reading my Bible more and more every day as I was searching for answers and understanding. I was building up hope and faith, knowing that it was because of God. I am a woman kept by God.

I had to do things that eased my mind. One of the things that I did was go fishing. Being near the water would soothe, calm, and relax me. I also started to do some of the positive things that I used to do like going for long walks, playing tennis, singing, and dancing. Me and Doug E. Fresh used to get down in my living room. More importantly, as I was going through my hurt and pain, I helped others that were going through it as well.

One thing is for sure; you will go through some stages of grief such as blaming. I blamed myself for my son's death because I couldn't get to him. I was in denial for a very long time, and I isolated myself. Then, there was the stage with the constant "what if" this and "what if" that.

The Purpose of Pain

Although the pain hurt really bad, I had to feel accomplished. I had to realize that the purpose of the pain was for a new birth to take place. I now advocate for victims that suffered a loss as I did. I have formed a group called T.K.O, which stands for "The PIT Maneuver Killed Our Loved One." We fight for the regulation of police chases. This group goes and lobbies in different cities, bringing about awareness that chasing and using the PIT maneuver terminates lives. We feel that it should be outlawed in the United States.

Since my son's accident and death, family members from all over have reached out to me wanting to help me ban the PIT maneuver. It is up to Congress whether or not to pass the Shonquell Bill for Justice: No Chase and No PIT in the United States.

I talked to families from Ohio, Texas, Georgia, North Carolina, and Tennessee. The purpose of my pain is to let families know that, although you are hurting, you still have a purpose. We all must go through a healing process. It's okay to grieve in your own way. Losing a loved one is something that you will never get over, but you have to find coping mechanisms.

You have to take tiny steps and do what you can to get through each day. Out of pain comes a new birth.

REMEMBERING SHONQUELL

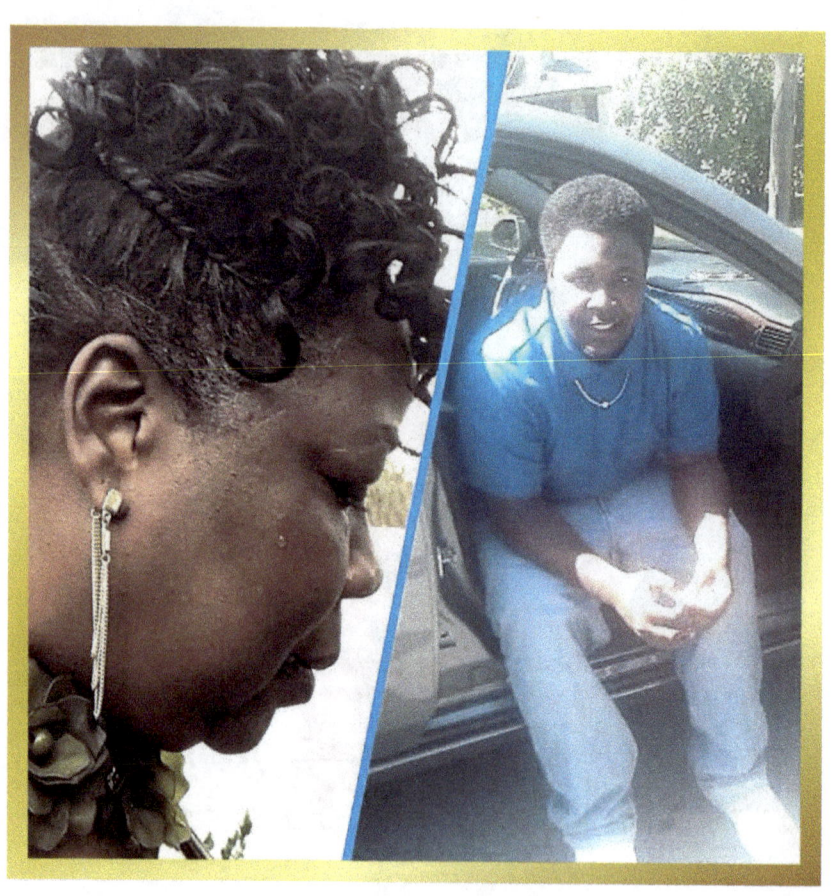

ABOUT THE AUTHOR

Charlene Ross was born in North Carolina. She always had a God-given gift, a love, and a passion for writing. Her creative penmanship displayed through her poems and church plays. Which allowed her audience to embrace her words and every part of who she is.

On the tragic and horrific night of June 29, 2018, Ross loss her firstborn and only son, Shonquell Barrett. With this magnitude of grief, she birthed her out of the pain, that led to the writing of this book. Which is her first of many.

Her heart's desire for this book is to help others deal with grief. It is a journey that you will have to walk alone. Charlene hopes to support grieving families that also lost a loved one due to the use of the PIT maneuver and chase. In her quest to get laws changed regarding the PIT maneuver, she has met with government officials. Also, several news media outlets throughout the United States have interviewed her on the topic.

Ross has often said, "Don't let time slip away." She strongly encourages others to live in the moment as she strives to do the same herself. Life is precious, so cherish your loved ones and make sure that your time is well spent.

Charlene currently lives in Aberdeen, North Carolina with her daughter Symphanie Barrett.

www.ingramcontent.com/pod-product-compliance
Lightning Source LLC
Chambersburg PA
CBHW051831160426
43209CB00006B/1126